FIFTEEN SECONDS WITHOUT SORROW

POEMS

Shim Bo-Seon

Translated by Chung Eun-Gwi &
Brother Anthony of Taizé

Parlor Press
Anderson, South Carolina
www.parlorpress.com

Parlor Press LLC, Anderson, South Carolina, 29621

Fifteen Seconds without Sorrow is published with the support of the Literature Translation Institute of Korea (LTI Korea).

Printed in the United States of America
S A N: 2 5 4 - 8 8 7 9

Library of Congress Cataloging-in-Publication Data

Names: Sim, Po-sæon, author. | Chæong, æUn-gwi, 1969- translator. | Anthony,
    of Taizâe, Brother, 1942- translator.
Title: Fifteen seconds without sorrow : poems / Shim Bo-Seon ; translated by
    Chung Eun-Gwi & Brother Anthony of Taizâe.
Description: Anderson, South Carolina : Parlor Press, 2016.
Identifiers: LCCN 2016028239| ISBN 9781602358355 (pbk. : alk. paper) | ISBN
    9781602358362 (pdf) | ISBN 9781602358379 (epub) | ISBN 9781602358386
    (iBook) | ISBN 9781602358393 (Kindle)
Classification: LCC PL994.72.P64 A2 2016 | DDC 895.71/5--dc23
LC record available at https://lccn.loc.gov/2016028239

Cover photograph by Shim Bo-Seon. Used by permission.
Printed on acid-free paper.

Parlor Press, LLC is an independent publisher of scholarly and trade titles in print and multimedia formats. This book is available in paperback and ebook formats from Parlor Press on the World Wide Web at http://www.parlorpress.com or through online and brick-and-mortar bookstores. For submission information or to find out about Parlor Press publications, write to Parlor Press, 3015 Brackenberry Drive, Anderson, South Carolina, 29621, or email editor@parlorpress.com.

FREE VERSE EDITIONS

EDITED BY JON THOMPSON

Contents

Translators' Preface

Chung Eun-Gwi and Brother Anthony of Taizé

Shim Bo-Seon made his poetic début in 1994 but he only published Fifteen Seconds Without Sorrow, his first collection of poems, fourteen years later, in 2008. This volume contains the poet's earliest, freshest poems reflecting a deep concern about the relationship between poetry and politics. His language, based on everyday life, is characterized by a very subtle feeling of the distance between fantasy and reality and an awareness of the difficulty of saying something significant simply. Raising philosophical questions about what it means to live as a human being in this world, his poems epitomize the doubts, values, and beliefs of individuals leading ordinary, secular lives.

As a poet-critic, Shim Bo-Seon fills his lines with the melodies of plain speech and subtle thinking about relationships in the world. Readers of Shim's poetry have often noted its wit and deceptive simplicity. His poems examine individual experiences and domestic details, playing these against the backdrop of contemporary Korean history. For Shim Bo-Seon, writing poetry is to imagine a commune, the space where people find some creative and constructive force for a better world. Writing in an allusive, indirect style about topics which are in themselves familiar, such as eating rice, taking off clothes, living in an apartment block, struggling with human relationships, Shim captures the sparkling moments of joy and sorrow, hope and frustration that are usually concealed in everyday death and life. The brief moments of recognition are invited to the new realm of spatial temporality of "fifteen seconds without sorrow," in which his language of the ordinary attains universal empathy for a poetic commune. In his modest and witty words, Shim Bo-Seon enacts circular movements of concealment, and revelations of the mysteries that an individual experiences are evoked in turn, usually lightly and sharply. As he has written:

> Sorrow and time are indispensable. Sorrow is confined by time. Sorrow is not everlasting but expands and multiplies, making a curve. As a poet, I try to keep going on, straight ahead, without thinking of the end. Poetry helps me to keep going forward without retreating backward. New forms of language make a new world and I get some comfort and energy from the process of making newness. When I write a poem, I usually start with an instant's feeling, an instant scene, or an image. For example, the poem, "Fifteen Seconds without Sorrow" was born when I happened to look blankly at a cat nibbling flower petals.

At the very moment, words sprang up from inside me and the words made certain images and then the world. That's how this poetry book was formed.

Shim's initial claim on the poetic subject is the world itself. His language is absorbed in the world as the world is absorbed in his language. When he follows the dictation of the ordinary landscape, it is to realize the foresight, prevision, and omens of the world. For him, the condition of talking and listening is basically being together in this world, even in its most skeptical stance. In terms of the ordinary, he faces its end and its anticipation. That's how he treads the way of the poetic world. In the process of translating his poems, we translators had some joy from being together with his mindscape and with the vivid nowadays' experiences and some sorrow from being apart from his casually shining words. But in translation, in which we struggle to find a way "out of nowhere," joy always defeats sorrow, so we are very happy to share *Fifteen Seconds Without Sorrow* with our readers.

FIFTEEN SECONDS WITHOUT SORROW

Evolutions of Sorrow

The world is absorbed in my language.
I realized that last night.
In my room, the silent desk is a long-term resident.

World!
Everlasting foul weather!
Give me edges like thunder!

If it had not been for sugar,
ants might have evolved into something rather bigger.
That was the sentence I completed after racking my brains all night.

(Then a long silence)

I keep getting fatter.
Like a desk that has lost its edges.

Here and there in this world, people are crying!
Even women born under Scorpio, who are said to be spiteful!

But I know nothing more about sorrow.
Just as a ball will never turn into a desk, even if it's given edges.

In that case,
what kind of furniture will human beings evolve into?
This was the question I completed after racking my brains all night.

(Then everlasting silence)

Parting after a Meal

Now we've finished one topic
it's time to part, dear.
I've grown tired of silent scenery.
Things that end up as they were before, no matter how much they're
    stirred,
things like rice gruel where the trail left by a spoon slowly
    disappears, for instance,
such things are no fun at all.

Streets change day and night curtly like a restaurant menu being
    opened then shut.
I'll vanish into that spreading darkness,
and you, turn your back, face the remaining brightness
and count to ten.
If you turn around after counting to ten,
the gums of the darkness that has swallowed me up
will softly touch your gentle cheekbones.

Good my dear,
eagerly eating the bullet I fired, aimed exactly at your heart,
as if it were a well-cooked grain of rice,
if there is a sound of good nature,
it is, for instance,
the sound you make inside as you slowly count to ten
while watching me quickly empty down a bowl of gruel,
a sound clearly heard though inaudible,
a sound that has to be heard at all costs,
the sound of a solid forehead being pierced and the mind's spiteful
    gruel being stirred.

That's what love is like.
It's like a strange famine in a strange country
where hunger never vanishes all year long
though every day yields a bumper harvest,
with left-over rice-gruel becoming cooked rice then that becoming
    raw rice again.
Now our strange old tale ends here.

Good my dear,
good my dear,
is the landscape over there still bright?
Is it still bright after I count to ten?
My ruins don't shine even if I count to a million billion.
I don't know how to bring up the soggy gruel of darkness.

Today, I

Today, like a trembling feather I have no goal.
Today, I am hiding behind things that have already vanished.
The sun, having lost morning's susceptibility,
glares in twilight's purple dignity.
Once the moon bears evening's rank pressed down on its head,
night will soon begin with the mournful expression of a passerby.
Black carcasses of birds I was indifferent to,
ash-hued segments drawn one by one on foreheads,
the sound of a neighbor hammering late,
other things like this and that.
Desperate about feelings and rules, I
forgot bygone times,
forgot dead friends,
forgot what agonies I was immersed in last year.
Today, I make a hole called the future in the calendar.
Next week's desires,
next month's void,
as well as requiems
of decisive nausea,
my share of tragedy, I know they still remain.
I know everyone has the right to hate.
Today I was scowling at someone's mournful face.
Today I began to love one woman.

A Ruin Very Briefly Shining

Like looking at pants I took off the day before,
I have no regrets about life.
If now I mean to start out on a long journey,
I should have got rid of my bitterly jealous heart before.
Glaring at the sun, I said I prefer square shapes.
Other shapes are all sad, I said.
After willows' shadows one by one lengthen
on the ash-hued wall as if grappling with the sun, night comes,
then she appeared, soon disappeared, like some ancient religion.
A few hairs on the bed after love-making,
objects that cannot find adequate metaphors, at times,
when I recall tragedy, a real tragedy would spread before my eyes.
Flowers never know the meaning of flower language,
but each bud was full of grief.
Life was full of lies at that time,
but a truth passing by the universe
borrowed the night's body, the moon's lips
and covered the western sky.
At that moment, looking like pants taken off somewhere,
shabbily crumpled life
was a ruin very briefly shining.
It was mighty and sacred.

Fifteen Seconds without Sorrow

Above a distant high-rise apartment
the sun is beating its breast,
at its wits' end beside the daytime moon.
Where shame is concerned, the world went to the dogs long ago.
Sometimes about fifteen seconds pass without sorrow.
Offering every possible excuse,
paths are bending everywhere.
The silence gathering on dusky sidewalks
hopes to grow older there by the second.
As they grow older, all beings leak when it rains.
All old beings that leak
dream of love like installing a new roof.
Everyone knows: whatever happens
was bound to turn out as it did.
One afternoon as the sun is squeezing out light with all its might,
the past goes walking backward and falls headlong
over the apartment railings. The future follows immediately after.
The present, being simply a flower's day, a flower's day
being the time it takes a flower to bloom and fall, is sad.
A cat is happily nibbling flower petals.
A woman is sipping chamomile tea.
They seem quiet and peaceful.
I stand aimlessly in the middle of the street.
A man passes by on a bicycle, weeping.
He is a human being destined to fall in the end.
The dream-garden in my head where dizziness is in full bloom.
Now about fifteen seconds have passed without sorrow.
I should set off somewhere,
but no matter where, ultimately, it's a disappearing path.

"Rubber Soul"

Nodding its head, the sun
has got this far. Men
brush aside their lovers'
long hair and step outside.
Rubbing sunshine all over their bodies like glue,
they head for some place worth

staying at. It's a winter's morning.
Their shadows are
like an overcoat worn once then thrown away.

When they walk,
one side of their breast gives out a crushing sound.
On their lips the froth from the last toast they drank
still remains. If their lover's
kiss is still sweet,
it's because of that. They have memories
like crushed beer cans.

In the places they left,
numerous strands of hair,
clumped together, are tumbling in the wind.
The windbreak windows of the lovers' rooms
are shivering *brrr*.
It's a winter morning.

The lovers of men who have left
are changing their underwear
at the lowest register.

*Rubber Soul: title of a Beatles album

Things That Lead Me to Disillusionment

The sun
The right
The smell of lemons
Strolling without a thought
A living dog beside a dead dog
An illustrated plant book without liverleaf
The last sentence in a religious book
Death on a slow screen
An artist's erudition
Losing by a wide margin
Temperamental people
Retrospectives
Citation and footnote
Yesterday's telephone conversation
Large bourgeois families
Pronouncing 'r' in French
My old school's main gate
Old lovers (in alphabetical order)
Consultants' concept of customer
Kant's Thing-in-itself
The term Thing-in-itself
The smell of lavender
Downward
Saturn

An Unavoidable Road

This road is the road I took yesterday too.
On this road, people
can only meet one other person.
Because of shame,
he pulls both ears down and covers his face with them.
But on this road,
there is nothing that cannot be mentioned.
All day long he lies face down.
In order to erase the shame,
he replaces his palms and face.
But yet, why are things that cannot be mentioned
unrelated to those that should be mentioned, why
don't rules become incidents?
This road is easy to remember.
The roadside trees succeed in
dropping their leaves all just at the same time.
In order to forget the shame,
he sometimes sings and
also claps.
He never says a word.
No one can greet him.

Scenery

1

A street after rain has stopped falling. Raindrops are collecting on the corners of the signboard of xx Service Center, falling and pooling. The afternoon silence is deep and shabby like the pockets of working clothes. Soon, the pooled water manages to pull at the edges of the world and soak into it. Then it moves up onto a well-dressed gentleman's leather shoes. The water quickly sponges off, leaving nothing but machine oil. Children see the oil congealed on the ground and stir it with their fingers, calling it a rainbow. A tenacious rainbow that has not been erased even after a week. . . . . perhaps it's a kind of patent.

2

At the pharmacy across the street, eczema and athlete's foot introduce themselves to one another. They shake hands, barely stretching them out as if squeezing ointment from a finished tube. I moved out here not long ago. Ah, I've been a native of this neighborhood for twenty years. Outside the pharmacy, the two stick out like hair at the same time. To think we are living so close like this. Let's tangle sometimes, hhhhh.... Replying with a smile when receiving greetings is correct behavior between neighbors. When evening comes, the street become the leg of a sleek shiny arthropod. Windows lighting up as prescribed.

3

Lights facing each another do not harbor malice toward one other. Rather, women occasionally check up by phone on their innocent seven-year-itch. The breadwinners have not come home yet. Like unfocussed eyes, the women are uneasy. The volume of waiting is always constant. If one side is pressed in resignation, the other side swells that much with dreams. The street lifts its feet and heavily moves toward midnight. Folded like document files, the breadwinners are returning home.

Going Shopping

One purebred Saint Bernard
is sitting at the entrance to a supermarket waiting for its master.
For a long time, not stirring an inch,
not once meeting anyone's eyes,
as if it had forgotten the Alps a long time ago.

Holding one garlic-flavored bagel,
estimating the size of its sturdy body inside the thick coat,
I stay standing in front of it for a while.
A whiff of garlic borne on the breeze,
its twitching wet nose tells of its outstanding health.

Twitching, like the shopping list my wife wrote down on the paper.
I wish the details of life could be tranquil and simple.
Twitching, the assurance given right before going shopping
—I'll select the highest quality meat –
though brief, is touching.

Finally, turning its head slowly,
the Saint Bernard stares at me.
The saliva hanging absent-minded about its lips is transparent.
You're awesome, real cool.
It's a bright day in early spring.
Hoping to be rescued by it, a blizzard is blowing
in the Alps of my mind,
as if I had forgotten about shopping a long time ago.

My Wife's Magic

My wife is sad and
seeing my sad wife, I too am sad,
then as she answers her mother's phone call, 'Sure, we're fine,'
the wife inside my wife grows sadder still.

I want to live in a world that's perfect like magic.
The rabbit that came out of a hat
voluntarily goes back into the hat.
When I try to go into a mirror,
I wonder why the rigid surface stops me?

A mother abandons her child,
a job abandons a father,
a disease abandons a sick person and
a magician finally abandons his rabbit.

If a heartless house kicks a road out the door, saying, "You, get out,"
an illusion takes the road, holds it tight then abandons it straight.

Wanting to dye the whole world with sorrow,
my crying wife is stroking the edge of the table on and on.
Curious magic that I see for the first time.

Moral and Aesthetic Meditation
Inside an Elevator

From time to time something clatters inside my body,
reminding me that there is something inside my body that clatters
   from time to time.

Immersed in my bath, I finished reading the whole volume of Hwang
   Ji-woo's poetry that my mother-in-law had sent from Korea.
On an inside page of the book was written: "To my son-in-law the
   poet who must be missing his native language."
(Actually, my mother-in-law's mistaken view of me as a poet with
   rather serious attitudes is a burden.)
Suddenly wondering how it might feel to read poetry in a weightless
   state,
I put the poetry book into the bathwater and turned the pages one by
   one.
Nothing could be smoother.
Some lines came bubbling up as foam and burst with a terrible smell
   on the surface of the water.

Emerging from the bathtub, I put on a bathrobe and thought:
Is it really ok not to be wearing anything underneath this?
Morally and aesthetically, is it ok? Besides,
can the existence of contemporary capitalism be justified?
That's a question I have been putting off answering for a long time.
   Or rather, in fact,
I wonder if I ever formulated such a question to start with?

While I was drying my hair with a hair dryer,
a call came from Mac, the social activist.
He's living with his girlfriend Lesley in her house, she's also a social
   activist.
He was asking me to come for supper in their place that evening.
(Actually, his mistaken view of me as a radical leftist from South
   Korea is a burden.)
It was only four o'clock yet inside the room it was already getting
   dark.
Like the way a revolution occurs when subjective conditions and

objective conditions match,
this room is brightest when the angle of the slats in the blind
    corresponds precisely
to the angle of the sunlight, but something like that
hardly ever happens to a lazy guy like me.

My wife, who never once took part in a demonstration when she was
    in college, gets on surprisingly well with my leftist friends.
Today she even asked if Arafat, another social activist, would be coming.
(Come to think of it, my wife even voted for the People's Party
    candidate in the last presidential election.)
And last time, when we sang "We Shall Overcome" all together in
    our place,
my wife kept silent and just laughed as she poured out green tea
    sitting beside me.
And yet, within the system known as marriage that conscientizes you
    about divorce,
my wife has hung in there for three whole years, cultivating me, a
    bad species of plant that never produces good-quality fruit.

Suddenly, I felt grateful, I felt like approaching my wife as she sat
    there in front of the computer and flashing my bathrobe open,
only I was not sure if such behavior could be approved, morally or
    aesthetically.
Getting up from her chair, as she adjusted the angle of the slats in
    the blind my wife complained:
I want to move to a brighter place.
But we need to think of the rent, you know, and you have to answer
    my question first!
Yet, what kind of question had I asked my wife? Indeed, had I ever
    asked her a question?
I could not remember, and while I was trying to remember, the
    sunlight moved beyond the critical level for the angle of the slats
    in the blind,
the room automatically grew dim, until soon everything was
    submerged in darkness.
In the darkness, a sound of something clattering from time to time
    could be heard,
reminding me that there was something clattering from time to time
    moving in the darkness.

When I woke up, surprisingly enough we were inside the elevator
  with the flickering light moving from 2→1.
Shouldn't we buy a bottle of wine to take to Lesley's house, and what
  on earth
are you thinking about so deeply like that? Beside me, my wife
  looked specially pretty today as she questioned me. Then
the elevator door opened wide like an outspread bathrobe, leading to
  another world.

Bread, Coat, Heart

Some men are sitting side by side on a park bench.
They do not look very amiable.
Their eyes are clearly tinged with red
as if they are mulling over a final deal with the devil.
Above their heads, a mass of dark clouds passes,
clearly denying the blueness of the sky.
Inside their dark coats
dark bread and dark hearts are enclosed.
How are bread and hearts alike?
They both grow black and hard with age.
But who knows?
Each of them might have an interesting story to tell.
For example, a fight involving a daughter,
or a merry episode related to a picnic.
Pigeons are circling nearby
watching out for regrets or disappointments
falling like breadcrumbs from their coats.
Pigeons cannot possibly know about metaphors.
Not saying a word,
the men are sitting in attitudes often seen in black-and-white movies.
I wouldn't be surprised if a subtitle "The End" were to rise lightly
in the air before their eyes.
The dark clouds move fast.
Like jobless people waiting for an evening food distribution,
red-faced they go flocking off into the western sky.
Those men look alike but they do not talk to each other.
They are each engrossed in their own thoughts.
And yet, who knows?
Once night comes, they may become the best of friends,
drinking together with arms around shoulders.
But now is a time for dark silence,
a time to ponder the reading of a cryptic future.
The pigeons, still not knowing about metaphors,
and not knowing how to give up, endlessly circle nearby.
From the bench they are sitting on, an unknown shadow
is spreading across the whole park.
It is, literally, the shade of unknowing.
The sun, in the midst of the sky lightly
floating, The End.

Illusion

Clouds taught me about ambiguity then went away.
Did poverty and hunger really mean that?
I hurriedly escape from the forces of discontent.
But they will remain my everlasting friends
even though we shed tears of different colors.
Tightly linked hands loosen calmly.
Is this a good sign?
Still, let's not change prayer into pleading.
Let's set fire to all the trouser-legs we want to hold onto,
flag, homeland, brothels, childhood alleys.
The revolution I once believed in will never come.
Rather, I will believe in ambiguous holiday weather reports.
A passing fox pats my shoulder, saying:
But think again.
Won't you be insignificant as well,
staying far away from all those things?
Now it's spring when flowers bloom abundantly ignoring distance.
So it is, and far off in the distance,
cherry blossom is dazzlingly beautiful.
Fox, I will now cast off knowledge and
choose obvious excitement and melancholy.
But think again.
Is that flower the sad flower you believed to be cherry blossom?
There's no way of knowing and saying there's no knowing
is neither more nor less than saying there's no knowing.
The passing fox passed on.
From here to truth is a very long journey.
I must keep going until that becomes obvious like puberty.
While poverty and hunger are a quite different matter.

Delusion Bus

I've lost my line;
bus line and political line,
I've lost them both.

The perishing world is more cheerful than I am
except for holidays and sex.

Sitting at the very back of a bus, I glare at the very front of the bus.
The bridge the bus is crossing now looks like a scar stretching to a
  vanishing point.
So that's good.

Leaning against a window, I fall into a doze.
A scattering of light swimming on the retina like a school of young fish.
Even in dreams, I cannot perform miracles.
Holding my breath patiently, I cross a river walking on the riverbed.

Looking back,
a former lover is walking lightly over the river.
I have lost the love that happened like a miracle.
Dream and reality,
both.

Passing many times through the same confession,
life produces colorful spectra.
Boredom is my rainbow.
My shadow is the exact opposite of light.
My language is the exact opposite of the exact opposite.

The bus speeds on in confusion.
Still it's good.

Downfall

Till now, I have never dreamt of jumping.
Only square doors have shifted me
from emptiness to emptiness
from flat surface to flat surface.
Existence is rolling down
slowly toward nonexistence
like an unmanned airship falling zigzag from the sky.
I was devoted to emotions,
discarded bad habits,
was not excessively greedy and maybe
I could have been a tall and handsome accountant.
And yet, what kind of vice dragged my life down this far?
Is it because of restless eyes and hesitant lips?
Is it because of a hundred friends and ten lovers?
I paid attention to all premonitions,
avoided heavy snowfall and rainfall as much as possible,
and believed that a decisive event,
either good or bad, would occur someday.
But not a damned bit of change came and
sunk in grief, watching a black and white movie
I merely cried: "Ohhh, that dazzling pink, pink!"
Could there be anything as unbearable
as finding oneself unbearable?
So I fell and
even at this moment, I am endlessly falling.
In this complicated, cruel street
where lost cats are bumming around with fur erect
and kindness is interpreted indifferently as an evil omen.

When We Were Boys and Girls

What honor do we still have left?
How many black knots in shadows do we still have left?
Do you remember?
When we were boys and girls,
the zoo at weekends always crowded,
elephants that used to shine like night-glow,
slow processions of camels and
the rapid progress of time,
years of coughs erupting like thunderbolts
as fruition formed, the so-called fist at the arm's end.
When we were boys and girls,
those were times of desiring half of one another, glancing sideways,
times of pickling puppy love in the shadow of flowers,
times of calling someone 'Silly you' and
responding 'Silly you.'
Do you remember?
If you remember,
laugh out loud.
Put out the golden horn sticking to your palate.
That's a second tongue made by long silence.
So you should know it well.
That laugh, it may sound loud,
it smells extremely bad.
We are sons and daughters of rotten hours.
We have no honor left.
Ultimately, all the black knots in shadows came untied.

I Laugh, I Have To

1.

Since father died,
there has been no high-flown talk in our family.
But under the blue fluorescent light,
my mom's basic English has improved day by day.

My mom asks me, What does 'nation' mean?
It means 'people'; it was a word Father liked a lot.
I see.
Ask me anything you like.
Does 'Tom and Jerry' mean 'cat and mouse'?
Ha-ha-ha, you joke more often as you get older.

I am the interpreter.
I am the oldest son who laughs loudly.
Even if tragedy strikes again,
even if there is no salvation anywhere,
I have to interpret exactly
and, finally, laugh loudly.

As the eldest son, simply as the eldest son,
I'll fight on until the bitter end
with our family's aimless, vague emotions,
unsure if they're pathos, or grief, or pity.

2

When I go speeding along the riverside on Father's bike, its tires
    flabby,
the landscape's tawdry reality gradually reveals itself.
Flowers bloom and wither,
snow drifts high then melts.
that's all.
And sometimes at shallow rapids
a white heron goes flying up, displaying glossy plumage.

Long ago I once buried a dead bird.
After that, wounded birds used to come and faint at my feet.
How charming, last words expressed only in chirping.

A bird, I don't know what it's called, staggers near,
blind in one eye.
If it were not for the chirping, birds' lively language,
it would be nothing but a black smudge whirling in the shadows,
   though.

3

I am walking with Mother in autumn sunshine.
Turning my hand palm-downward, the back of my hand gleams bright,
the word "warmish" means "warmish,"
"the rest of my life" means repeating autumn, winter, spring, summer
   a number of times.

When I ponder the strange connection between wounded birds and
   myself
in the autumn sunlight,
the world grows impossibly still.
It may be lonely, may be sad, but Mother's heart keeps beating pit-
   pat, pit-pat.

I've heard that a suicide shouted, Jump!
as he threw himself off the roof of a building.
His heart must have beat an irregular pitta-pat, pitta-pat
cheerfully until the moment it stopped.

but other people's things abandoned in the shadows,
those very common palms and hand-backs,
are awkwardly enduring the rest of their life as cold air spreads clearly.
It's a thing to be endured. It has to be, surely.

4

Tell me where there is meaning apart from people and language.
I will dwell there, spending all the seasonal seasons that remain.
But I must feel pathos, grief, pity, for the things already given me
as of now are all there are.

Ah, black smudges came and went beneath my feet.

In sunlight or in shadows
I laugh, I just have to laugh
for the things already given me
as of now are simply all there are
as of now.

Peaceful Holiday

Today is a holiday.
The morning was peaceful.
My nephews watched "Tom and Jerry."
My younger brother and his wife laughed quietly.
My younger sister drank a cup of weak coffee.
Mother grew a very little bit older.

Today is a holiday.
The afternoon is peaceful.
My second nephew asks when his uncle will get married;
judging by his question, he must know about divorce.
From the way my first nephew stands in front of his father's death-
portrait
without a word, he seems to know about death.

Today is a holiday.
Hopefully, it will be peaceful all evening long.
There are two missed calls.
I call to mind your beauty.
I call to mind beloved you.
Suddenly I start to wonder about the scenery outside the window.
If it's empty sky, I want to jump down and
if it's clouds, I want to jump up.

Today is a holiday.
A peaceful day like this
is unlikely to come again.

Two

Two sunbeams
Two prongs of time
Two verses of dream
Two times looking back
Two emotions
Two people
Two steps
Two directions
Only two kinds of event exist.
One is possibility.
The other is nothing.

If It Were Not for Songs

Life with its many defects listens meekly to the wind humming on the road of songs. What profound secret of combing makes songs spread the history of humiliation like a girl untying her hair ribbon? If it were not for songs, humanity could never even have dreamt of life's perfection. A river carved numerous wavelets on its body like a set of tattoos. Erasing them, it flows into the sea. Life's perfection is also like a moiré fringe pattern that a song's melody left by chance on the edge of a dream; a person needs to connect the heart's texture to that and preserve every single part of the old song's history. At the same time, people need to cross each age's plateau with the life of a melody. Then the song will see them off at this life's last entrance with a warm-hearted elegy: "Oh, dear, oh, dear, let's cross over, oh, dear." In this weird land of fire every desire glows crimson and the only things that will not burn until the day they turn into black ashes are songs. Really. It must be like that. If it were not for songs, we could never have dreamt of life's perfection.

Acrobat of Clouds and Fogs

Apart from clouds and fogs, I do not have much to talk about.
When I elucidate those two, my body is soaked with a pleasant-
feeling strangeness.
I tried to sublimate that into a dazzling acrobatic display.
An emcee once asked me how I managed to make a perfect circle by
bending backwards.
I felt like eating fresh shit, of course.
As I gave a demonstration on the spot, the audience clapped and
vomited too.

I gave up studying and working by immersing myself in clouds and
fogs long ago.
In the places where I jumped up and down, pubic hair used to pile
up in heaps.
Was that because an important part of my body was gradually
turning into clouds and fogs?
Anyhow, if you want to find out my whereabouts, you only have to
follow the strands of hair that have fallen to the ground.
I am just a solitary acrobat.
Joys and sorrows are my only morality.
Love and confessions are absolutely forbidden.
As for what my name is and where my residence is, that is absolute
silence.

I sometimes strut down streets by night and look at my reflection in
the display windows.
I am reflected back at myself as a distant abyss and
until the darkness behind my back and the light in front of my eyes
welcome each other,
I stay standing there for a long time, with the poorest expression of a
whole lifetime.
Then, sunk in a profound mood, I walk on my hands toward the spot
where the moon rises.
Midnight streets are always crowded with drunken men and
prostitutes.
You people bathed in the moonlight passing through my round body,
whether you laugh at me or adore me, may your lives be full of
fecundity and good fortune.

Sometimes, I run on and on, piercing clouds and fogs.
When clouds and fogs lift, I get bored and come straight back home.
A street where clouds and fogs have lifted is
a teacher without knowledge,
a face with no expression.
Solitude gains a beautiful figure when it is trimmed with clouds and
    polished with fog, I believe.

I am just a solitary acrobat.
If I particularly mention a school,
I am of the 'cloudy weather' school studying the shapes of thick fogs
    and clouds in the streets of mind.
Since solitude has been from ancient times a mystery that looks
    beautiful only to itself,
it does not cling to the praise, contempt and indifference of others.
Joys and sorrows are my only morality.
Love and confessions are absolutely forbidden.
As for how I have lived and how I will live, that is absolute silence.

You

You achieved what I could not achieve.
You seduced my failure and brought it to success.
You organized effectively the end of art and corrupted language and
    wet desire and the crumbling world and the impossible future.
(in just one sentence, at that!)
Thus you gained limitless freedom regarding the world.
Then you accomplished the unspeakable, that had been lavishly
    expanding like an extended family.
As a peerless poet, as a singer with a noisily throbbing heart,
first you manifested a perfect fall, then manifested a more perfect
    resurrection.
Born in a landscape then erasing the landscape,
changing the essence after reaching the essence,
you are the incarnation of a legendary Chinese wizard.
When I feel jealous, you are sad;
when I express respect, you laugh it off magnanimously,
You often embrace me.
You impress me every time.
Focal source of the rumor that raised me,
hermaphrodite, father and mother in a single body,
half-man-half-beast, combining bird-like lover and lover-like bird,
yes,
the time has come at last.
I am leaving you.
You are not me.
I do not know you.
Now, farewell.

A Rumor I Cannot Deal With

I am a rumor about myself. I am an ominous word that death whispers in life's ear. I live in fear and trembling. My demeanor is dark as pitch.

It is the future that always comes, even when it does not seem to be coming. The future always emerges from somewhere like a monkey and holds out its hand. It's extremely unpleasant. I much prefer to avoid it.

The things that passed through my heart long ago seem to have gathered somewhere to form a bright, round nation. There walks, sunshine, songs, and moonlight will be connected with fine gold threads. Everyone will have a graceful shadow bestowed on them by a giraffe. They will speak using nothing but easy and transparent words. Making a fuss will be the only tragic situation.

Beneath life's fragile sky, that might shatter like rice puffs at the slightest touch, there is nothing that I have given birth to, fed, and raised. Absolutely nothing. How on earth did these poor things get their names?

So, what on earth should I do? This rumor, circling about my ears, droning, unending, saying that I am alive; what on earth should I do about it?

The Myth of the Child

A strange myth is drifting around where the moon sets. Likewise where the sun rises. It says that children suddenly became grown-ups after having created the world for 7 days.

As one of those children, I feel nothing but extreme anxiety and sorrow. Roaming around inside all that imperfection, I murmur nothing but utter anxiety and sorrow. Like other children, I created a world where simple curiosity became the loftiest altruism and solicitude with the help of a fickle god at the age of five, then, as a very manly and scary grown-up, I ordered all my neighbors and myself to forget that god. In my dreams that god sometimes appears, grinding his one-hundred-and eight teeth, then runs into someone else's dream and dances joyfully. He really is what you would call a fickle god, isn't he? Most of the roads in my world are a labyrinth. Only one of the roads is not a labyrinth, and that is the road of letters. Everywhere in my world, entrances to the labyrinth disguised as entrances to bars, restaurants, libraries, schools, etc. open their big mouths wide. In that labyrinth live monsters, half-beast-half-man, disguised as bartenders, chefs, librarians, teachers, etc. opening their big mouths wide. The real bars, restaurants, libraries, schools, etc., are in books and the real bartenders, chefs, librarians, teachers, etc., are people reading those books in the loneliness of the sexagenary cycle. (Of myself who resort to this trite dichotomy I speak as follows: I am immature as a person, unrefined as a writer, ignorant as a philosopher. However, as a creator I exist in myself – I AM WHO I AM [Exodus 3:14], so I am unaffected by the doubt and anguish brought on by all that imperfection).

The moon sets in my breast. The sun rises between my legs. I am not someone born on the earth but someone left after the earth has been burned. I am the the ultimate void left after everything has disappeared. Not a bright relief, I mean, but a black intaglio. In order to write my biography, I should read every myth in the world, spend my whole life immersed in grief and then, having died, be born in my next life as the best of biographers. But bear this in mind: I am also the one who bestows such a destiny.

Dust or Ruins

1.

The world lies flat, wearing a mask of ruins. Below, there is an abyss imagining ruins. To reach the abyss, would you gladly become the abyss? But bear this in mind: it is not you who imagine the world, it is the world that imagines you. You are just another ruin that the world has made, another mask, and seen globally, your sorrow is nothing more than a personal taste. Therefore, rather than the impossibility of trying to resemble the abyss, you should dream of the possibility of being a mask resembling the abyss's wrinkles, echoes, and colors.

2.

A father who passed away sitting down.
A mother crying hidden inside a wardrobe.
A dog that never barks.
A tree withered into the shape of a backbone.
Things that become a sandstorm when mixed together and rubbed
    in the hands.
Bristly phantoms.
Things that become fascinating only after I turn and look away.

3.

If I press hard on the edge of a memory, one blurred scene is printed
    out like a Polaroid photo. I'm a being who leaps and shakes his
    whole body till that grows sharp.

After believing in fate,
cursing salvation,
lusting right after humiliation,
scowling at the sun while longing for the moon,
dancing joyfully to an imaginary, unaccompanied rhapsody,
it's
ultimately a matter, that's right, perfectly, fatally, of falling over.

4.

This type of people spend their whole lives trying to find an identity, asking, who am I and where is my life headed? With their introverted and sentimental temperament they worry about something inwardly, then when they make a decision they become unusually decisive, disconcerting those around them. (INFP, description of the so-called explorer type, according to MBTI personality analysis).

5.

What lies between morning stillness and afternoon wind?
Irreversible time.
The reason why flowers bloom impetuously and trees die slowly.
Well, something of that kind, whatever,
the meaninglessness of a brief instant
becoming magnificent for a moment,
or
a brief instant of meaninglessness.

6.
"I would like to come back to a subject of which I have already spoken, the continuous creation of unforeseeable novelty which seems to be going on in the universe. As far as I am concerned, I feel I am experiencing it constantly. No matter how I try to imagine in detail what is going to happen to me, still how inadequate, how abstract and stilted is the thing I have imagined in comparison to what actually happens! The realization brings along with it an unforeseeable nothing which changes everything."
(Part of Henri Bergson's "La Pensée et le Mouvant," that she read to me one day over the phone.)

7.

Therefore an alchemist once had to turn back into stone within a hundred days all the gold that he had made throughout his whole life in order to be allowed by God to spend just one ordinary day being able to eat, to drink, to sing, to doze. For that one ordinary day was for him much more miraculous than all miracles he had performed in his whole lifetime.

8.

What I wanted was just one perfect love. Things like a perfect human being or a perfect epigram were easily completed by a joke at the end of a meal. Even to a common mortal like me, the revelation of love came down one day, awakened poetry in me and made me dream of ruins.

(You live with love in your mouth like a spoon. If you are hungry, come on, gobble me up.)

You stayed with me, the love of my life, and now you are leaving.
As you leave, only remember my lips' secret motion,
every single phrase of the tongue lying flat behind my lips and
    wailing.
Oh, if only I could turn the clock back!
Flowers bloom impetuously and trees die slowly.
Until the seasons with their innumerable changes have been finely
    ground up
and turned into days of dust scattered throughout the universe with
    no place to stay,
I will remember you

9.

And so, just as the first dust is born as the second after eons of reincarnation, even if there are seasons of elephants, high mountains, and seas between dust and dust, there is no life that is not afraid when faced with extinction, not embarrassed when faced with immortality..

10.

One who has lost love dreams of love again, one who has lost language dreams of language again, that's all.

A Hungry Father

A plant that grew up on a diet of rice-gruel
is making empty rice bowls blossom.

On reflection,
what has ruined me is mere gluttony; because of hunger
every night with my palms
I have made plaster casts of a woman's breasts shaped like rice bowls

Hey, world, I'm hungry.
I hold out to you my palm that is about to be broken.
Hey, world, this kind of gesture is now the last.

The sun is pouring down light
like gruel onto petals.

No matter how much I reflect,
what has ruined me is mere gluttony.

Oh, my poor daughter,
come here quickly.
I want to cover your scanty cliffs in a mouthful.

I, I am your frightful father.

My Dancing Queen

I remember the coarse texture of this fake leather couch.
My hand was caught between that woman's ass and the seat
like a dead butterfly. That was ten years ago.
I wonder why my life turned out like this, I said,
and at that she fell in love with me.
It's been a long while, and still you're crazy.
Because I'm a dancer. For a dancer, being crazy is nothing special.
She easily falls in love with nonsensical words.
I say something but my words are buried
in the ponderous texture of ABBA's *Dancing Queen*.
That woman dances like one really crazy bitch, and the music
coils round me, sucks at my ear before I can even unzip.
D minor's long tongue pierces my eardrum and touches my brain.
(I wonder what my brain tastes like).
If I ask the buoy floating above my brain,
Are you lonely?
it merely bobs in the waves of the words 'are you lonely?'
The buoy has no answer. Of course.
Just bobbing is the buoy's reason for being.
Anyway,
to the question, why did my life turn out like this?
there is no truth. There was no truth anywhere from the beginning.
Why do people fall in love?
Probably because, since there's no truth, they are mortally anxious.
The strobe at the strip club sprays light all over the place,
tatatata, like bullets.
Just as *tatatata* is life's only background music
for the angry young gangster belonging to the "Angry Youth Gang,"
I am mad about music. She
looks happy to have met me.
Clutching the pole and plucking her back, that's arched like a bow,
she's shooting seductive smiles at the audience.
Her dance steps resemble a butterfly.
They say only things that are easily torn can float in the air.
Goodbye, farewell, whether you stay crazy or not.
I come out of the bar, walk along damp dawn streets,
jump over the park fence

and arrive at the field inside my head.
There, a single tree is standing alone,
I am a gardener reunited with the tree after ten years.
Wearing overalls, holding a pair of secateurs in my hand,
looking deeply moved, I stand in front of the tree.
If I ask the tree, Are you lonely? that's silly,
just as it's silly to ask a stripper, Are you lonely?
All she needs is a change of underwear and tips (lots of them).
Love is but a cheeky (dead) butterfly.
What might the tree inside my head need?
I want to do something for it,
really, I want to do something
but I don't know what to say.
The tree in my head, being just a tree,
is simply completing a philosophical disco.
For my entire life, it has simply been raising a single branch
    diagonally
very slowly from below my left waist to above my right waist.
What does that mean? From here to eternity?
Anyway,
The tree inside my head is the only being I love,
standing there even after I'm dead,
my karma,
my
everlaaaasting
Dancing Queen!

A Poem in -ing

How are you doing? Where are you going? Don't say you don't know me and start leaving. Was it in a PC café, our first meeting? No, perhaps in a previous stage of being. How are you keeping? Sad, I'm feeling. Today I broke up with my darling. Would you believe that the leg I've been stroking, the leg I caressed for the last six months each evening, was a wooden leg in a stocking? That's what yesterday I ended up learning. I'm a bastard, you're thinking. Direct upward your looking. That stupid moon dangling. Up there since noon for fear someone else might steal its seating. That's foolish, I'm thinking. A hundred years were passing. How's your remembering? Your father 'mother' I used to be calling. Always befriending. Brother, father, are names I'm not using. Everyone 'mother' I've been calling. My life is only a comic meeting. The Hong Gil-Dong story and the Oedipus myth blending. Who the hell are you, you'll be asking. A few lifetimes have gone passing. We belonged to the same lazy country's national team for strolling. Aren't you recalling? You asked why we were living. You said you were feeling absurdly lonely like a kidnapper in a world with no kids for kidnapping. Was it French or Spanish you were speaking? You were using a language that seemed to squeeze all the world's absurdity into the 'r's you were pronouncing. That was my thinking. After the very first life, every following life is just refrain-repeating. What I'm thinking? God is a DJ mixing into an infinite version every kind of human feeling. And we human beings just dance as the rhythm's dictating. What about a cup of coffee or something? Oh, please no cream-pouring. I get upset watching white stuff spread like clouds billowing. Shall we call it excessive sensitivity to blatant sexual imagining? Whom are you awaiting? That's a blessing. How are you doing? I have recently once again taken up poetry writing. The fact is, I just call it a poem whenever I write anything. The other day, I attached a photo to an application form and claimed it was a poem, not an application form, or something. I reckon getting a job might to be possible after a few lives' passing. Do I look like some weird kind of being? Your expression indicates you have an uncomfortable feeling. No worrying. I won't keep you from leaving. The coffee's on me...unless you're insisting. Must you be going? Sorry to have kept you waiting. Well, see you in another life, I'm hoping. Or if not, nothing.

A Thousand-Year-Old Metaphysician

If illusion meets knowledge, there's nothing but pain.
Consider his life, as he sits on the chair, severely mutilated.
In the course of a thousand years so much has changed.
The number of stars has doubled while the moon has merged with
    the earth.
The days for refining solid beauty are over.
The white hands that neatly packaged salvation are gone.
Hearts have became all soft and confused
so that pleasure, courtesy, and wisdom are not distinguished.
For a thousand years he has been sitting on the chair at the will of
    the chair.
On the nearby hills, flowers are blooming like laughter bursting out
after being held back for a thousand years.
Long ago, he went for a walk along that hillside trail with his now
    dead wife
He smokes one final cigarette.
It does not matter what happens now.
In the heart even bad blood does not flow.
A postman called him old printed matter,
the coroner called him an amputated piece of body.
He thinks he is becoming the ghost of the chair.
His body, detached from the chair
and transferred to the box labeled 'unclassified,'
will spend the rest of its days in eternal darkness.
Just before the cover of the box is closed
he cries out with all his might,
Long live metaphysics, the will of the chair!
But no one lends an ear to his words.

Hands Becoming Normal

A white hand, a pale hand,
a hand like a disappearing galaxy
seen out of focus,
is stroking a woman's face.
The woman is sitting on the sofa like a Pensive Bodhisattva.
As if to say she has regained this posture at the end of lengthy rebirths,
after a thousand years,
as if to say nobody can take this posture from her,
the owner of the hand says, 'Thank you.
That is one more reason why I should live after meeting you.'
The man's hand is like a lotus flower blooming on the woman's face.
The woman's face is tranquil like a pond.
They would have moved from two to three or from three to four,
something like that.
For some reason, each piece of furniture in this room
seems to be cherishing an unspeakable sadness,
like a temple enshrining a relic of Buddha just after Buddha has walked out.
Now you will walk out too.
As soon as the man opens the door and walks out
the woman starts to age.
It is as if she will go on aging for ever
siting on the sofa cross-legged reflecting on parting
in the same posture,
for the man has gone and will not come back.
The man had daily use of love
but never gave up so much as a single hair of his life.
The man will recall his love with the woman
like what he thought was the clearest line in his palm
being really a deeply etched scar,
like having a memory of the hand having hurt badly,
though he could not recall
what he had grasped or cut.
It didn't matter
whether love was called
sublime inspiration
or brutal curse
or whatever else.
That was it.
After that parting, the man's hand became more and more normal,
like the brow of a monk who has returned to the world losing its light.

On Religion

1.

It's a bright spring day just past the end of the century.
A sweeper with ears blocked is sweeping up failed metaphors
and clouds of pollen are scattering aimlessly in all directions.
Those minute words plotting tears, since now
is an age in which allergies outdo religion,
destruction and salvation have become really simple.

2.

You should at least once have sent some news;
I felt so lonely that I hoped to be infected by some disease,
then late yesterday I went to the riverside, idled there before coming
     home.
Like writing paper in the envelope you sent back,
finely torn strips of moonlight were flowing over the ripples,
and I felt inclined to convert one by one to each of the constellations
floating densely in the night sky.
In order to forget you, I have changed religion several times.

3.

The prodigal son who left home in the morning
is coming back home for supper.
As evidence of his wandering his whole body is thick with pollen,
and when I go out into the desert, Father, my eyes sting so.
My boy, that's no desert, it's just a playground in a park.
In any case, once I go out tomorrow, I won't come back.
What is needed is not firm promises but a few credit cards.

4.

Mystery of life, shattering and scattering like pollen!
Despairing godhead stretched blooming on the cross.
Now a variety of souls is dwelling in every corner of my body.
All so trivial. All so innocent.

The Last Dessert

Like someone sitting askew on a chair, the sun is straddling the horizon.
Darkness is spreading like wine spilled onto a table.
The stars, hurtling toward extinction, are fearfully bright.
Even the creator, who once walked the halls of the universe, has
    stood to one side.
There is something musical about the shore's lassitude.
As wave strums wave, they break white.
Beyond the horizon, it's said, lives the god of wine who brews liquor
    as twilight.
Ships loaded with humans' stinking greed hover round the local
    shores.
I wonder if the Twelve Apostles at the Last Supper could finish all
    the food and drink.
Seeing Peter with his keen appetite, Jesus felt a surge of anger.
An intensely bitter taste will dominate the back of your tongue for
    ever.
I believe that every future is a fatal mistranslation of today.
Now it's time to decide whether to have dessert or not.
Above the horizon that barely divides black ocean from black sky,
the full moon is pale as the face of Judas when he pushed back the
    chair and stood up.

Once He Envied the Life of a
Golden Telegraph Pole

Time creases his face
a little more every day in passing.
Increasingly crumpled day by day,
one day he'll be able to wipe death's behind really well.

Like a Kleenex tissue, wonderfully soft.

Time spreads wrinkles like booby traps round his eyes
every day in passing.
If you're caught there and brought down

it's horrible! Early one evening as the sun was setting

he once envied from afar
the life of a golden telegraph pole staying on the horizon.

Night Deepening in Pastoral Mode

Once this forlorn and silent evening is over
night will come, when I start wanting to prattle a host of aphorisms.
Ah, if just one of them could get close to being true!
Across the time of all the stars that wander the darkness of the
    heavenly vault,
the moon once again rises clearly in human hearts.
Is what we call Eternity
nothing more than a dead baby rat
that Minerva's owl gnaws at bit by bit?
Now Earth's night
is deepening as a mere pastoral mode
while the buzzing of night insects between song and silence
and low whistles calling old dogs home
strike the deaf ears of a village patriarch dying alone.
One sheep, two sheep, three sheep,
pushing them over a cliff one by one, he falls asleep.
Though should someone somewhere start telling a story about a
    human being
he'll open his eyes wide, even while sleeping.

Outside of That

Outside of that, it is said the wind is always blowing.
It is said that palm groves are covered with thick fog and beyond that,
    the sea,
the broad sea extends.
Outside of that,
it is said, lies a dark civilization recorded by the barking of wild dogs.
There, it is said, a storyteller who has lost human speech
never blames himself for his long-lasting silence.
Eternity, it is said, after shaking hands with primal time
gained arms so long that no fingertips can be seen.
Every night, we have to squat in a damp, smelly inside
and greet the future as it comes running like a crowd of hunchbacks.
Ah, Time, give me one of your fastest arrows and with that
I will hit the unknown center coiled in the air outside.
When it comes to the outside that is not the inside
we are marksmen of unfailing precision,
or prophets.
Outside of that, it is said,
tomorrow's most sinister flowers in abundance
will burst into bloom in great abundance.

Blow, Wind!

Blow, wind, you are a baby boom transcending time, from dust's despair to typhoon's revolution, giving birth without hesitation, your arrogant, prolific flesh, my acute mental indigestion when faced with that, a sense of inferiority appallingly heated to boiling point, and while someone dreams of the wind's frontier, the wind harvests that person's shame; come, wind, from far away, a black band bound around your head, come running like a long distance runner; on the day when we meet you, hair waving even without you, flags fluttering even without you, life's long-cold heart will embrace hot peace; amazement! even though gales blow, each fallen leaf finds exactly its shadow and settles there with unfailing precision, fallen leaf, fallen leaf, trivial miracle of slender trees, miracle, miracle; blow, wind; and even though the wind blows, someone, in the wind, like the beating wings of a mayfly that worships immortality, is living, must live, cannot but live.

The Relationship between Nature
and Me Since the 18th Century

A mountain peak that stood naked all winter long has now slipped on a green bra. Ah, Nature! Ever since the 18th century, I have been unhappy. I rowed this far with my dick as an oar. Looking back, I see the water is torn here and there. Ah, Nature! Flowing wound! Old comrade! I wash my dirty hands in the waves of the gasping, breathlessly melting ice. I have never felt such a warm hole before. Indeed, ever since the 18th century, history has been an artificial forest made with grafted dicks. The road that starved all winter long is now chewing the warm breeze's song like fodder. Ah, Nature! Torn musical score! Unique maternity! Crouched at the riverside, I bend my dick into an 'L' shape and begin to grind it on a whetstone until it becomes a sharp sickle. Before long a spring day will pounce on me from behind my back, laughing aloud like a wild fire.

Youth

When you spat a gobbet of feigned evil at my face in the mirror and laughed aloud, when you went racing ahead of that woman with your hair disheveled like a boast, when you seized your father's collar in a burst of anger then an instant later let go again trembling in fear, when you made innumerable decisions staring hard at strangers across the river, when you begged your friend to curse at you as you enjoyed letting things go in one ear then out the other, when you tore off part of your most confident mind and tried to make a perfect body with it, when you gulped down humiliation like milk every night then fell asleep and your dreams grew much taller, when it seemed you could spend your whole life in command of the shadows between street lamp and street lamp that divided each into several shadows, when saying I love and saying I'm collapsing totally were the same, when you honestly speaking secretly admired intact life without pain, when therefore you wanted to just drop dead because you so much wanted to live, such is youth, that we term the flowering fresh green spring that comes just once in a lifetime.

In my Thirties

I was grown up. In my thirties, youth had been chewed and discarded like gum. Sometimes tears fell but I did not believe that was a miracle. Merely taken by surprise, I used to make phone calls to friends, How are you doing? Taking walks was my religion, yawning was my prayer, how good that I have something to believe in. I used to go out to the park and take photos, eat *gimbab*. It was a peaceful time, my thirties, but is peace so reliable? Lying on the lawn, I would watch the sky scratched by vapor trails healing in a flash. White blood pooling somewhere inside me, you appeared in a dream. In the next day's dream you were standing in the same place. Drawing closer, I saw it was a bird resembling you. (Please, don't fly away.) It's my thirties, I'm fully grown, why am I living? Does love still come? Does it still hurt? Does my body still shake with fever? This empty room when I come back from a walk, if someone merely drops in, spits, the leaves, the season will be warm. Choosing some music, making tea, turning the pages of a book, watering the potted plants, if you call that kind of thing a cozy holiday, well, okay, and outside the window autumn rain is falling. In my thirties, watching raindrops flow for a long, long time, alive or not alive, I am living.

Song of a Golden Sleeve

Memory! While I went wandering down dark alleys in search of you, you were already leaning at the end of the cul-de-sac inside me, tapping its end on your palm then skillfully lighting a cigarette. Grief! Song endlessly ablaze in beings soaked with rain and so not burning well. There is an invisible good fortune in every exile.

Hovering between music scores with a handful of starving mind, I often peeped. Memory! you were always an unknown song. If you fold the outside, the inside gets crumpled. A friend who fell into despair after joining the army killed himself but a friend who joined the army after experiencing despair survived. Even if I fold the inside dozens of times, the outside does not get crumpled at all.

In spring, with bare trees slowly adjusting their waistlines, just before I fell, little violets always came flocking. I knew that tears are the form of your song, just as the juice ejected by flowers as they decay is the form of floral language. Memory! I don't know where I should flee to. Running away from home would be a happiness... On the inside there is no outside, or rather, there are too many outsides.

There was a prolonged blackout. In that time I gathered the darkness into a ball beneath my bent back and ran for my life. The last wounds. Standing at the edge of the still less than healed mudflats, I looked at the vast skin that covered them as far as the horizon. The muscles of the song that drew in the waves, bulging more at a low note. Ah, Memory! Now with my arm I will roll up one of your arm's golden sleeves.

Every Time I Pass This Place

There, a pharmacy, inside, my, friend's mother, red and blue, colorful mosaic, inside, a person, the lower half of whose body, I, have never seen, floating about, all day long, smiling when she sees me, the only, prescription, in my teens, a private, superstition, a person, a person, illness on one hand, a pill on the other hand, taken for a long time, rubbing both hands together, spilling on the ground, the fine, solid, lines of the palm, mother, only called mother, the easiest, the saddest word, that, person, before, one is aware of it, piles up, piles up again, a hill, of language, a desire, never, able to overcome, a person, a faint shadow, inside, the body, that dragged at me, a dark truth, whenever I passed this place, decisive, fatal, that, laugh, laugh, that, barely escaped, that, glass cave, of smells, inside, the beginning of the world, the end, the border, that, woman, a person, ah, trivial, so very

Happy Birthday

Again and again I see an apparition, and beyond the apparition, I see an apparition, again and again I see an apparition, beyond the apparition, beyond the apparition, I see an apparition that is changing its clothes. I see an apparition again and again beyond an apparition, beyond an apparition, an apparition, ... beyond, I see innumerable apparitions.

Whenever I look back at friends I have taken a picture of they are still standing frozen there saying 'cheese.' On my face, there's a scratch made by a handful of coarse salt. For the first time in a decade, I wipe away sweat. The girl I broke up with in my sophomore year is still there in the café, holding a cup of cold coffee in her trembling hands. I wrote my will on some spilled water and even signed it. When the words, 'Drop dead,' had evaporated, I was finally drunk on lightness. I know how to cry and I know how to laugh, and I can choose between the two within ten seconds. My facial expression is like a record of the last resistance of an urban guerrilla. And the last world I risked my life for is within a hundred steps in every direction from where I am standing right now. Get out, everybody. Today's my birthday.

The World Is Delicious

While he was just singing about himself,
while he was concentrating like that, I
went for a stroll far away and returned.
The after-effects are serious.
The increasingly worn-down world's ins and outs were sad.
The way the world's going bust, lonesome weather,
is entirely
the fault of its temperature's lack of body heat.

Now he has become a hypocrite.
Confronted with scenery, he pretends to be a third person, but
the scenery only moves when there's life.
Otherwise, it simply sways at most.
When life approaches him,
he'll be puzzled, he'll be scared,
like a fool, like a foooool.

Once so deeply respected by me, he
is now completely at a loss,
squinting his eyes
in front of the birthday cake I brought him as a gift.
This is the world! The world comes first!
As I shout, he grabs a piece of cake
and throws it at me with all his strength.
While I am thinking

of that as part of earth's movement,
soft ins and outs cover my face.
Crushed cake is still cake.
It's sweet.
It's the taste of the world.

Growth Record

1.

Now I am wondering how many times I should fold my will.
I was very young but
my surroundings are full of old and ageing secrets.
To them I deliver my last sermon.

2.

After that
I grew up.
I went to market following Mother
I went back home following Mother
In the yard of our house, a larch tree stood.
When the wind blew, the branches wildly made the sign of the cross.
Like the tree, I also had limbs that were too far
removed from the roots. One day,

a shadow oozed from the tips of my toes. One day,
just as I awoke, a bird flew flapping away,
it had been pecking at my navel.
I often walked to Yeoido pushing my bicycle.
On my way back, crouching on the landing
I counted how many times my shadow could be folded. After that

I grew up.
I often picked up objects I saw for the first time lying on the street.
I always cried or laughed in just the right places.
I could tell whether to laugh or cry by observing the shadows.

3.

Now I am feeling wretchedly ashamed.
Now I am wondering how many times my will will be unfolded.
Thinking was my chronic illness.
And still sitting on the same chair,
I have confessed too many things to them.

Madman's Road

On the road, I grew frightened. Even in broad daytime, darkness was teasing me. While I slept last night I munched a dream that was still not ripe. In the morning, I found the flowers I had arranged in the vase had all been torn out. Instead of stomach acid, flower sap came welling up and the soles of my feet were furred. My steps, stammering, confessed to leaving footprints. I grew frightened. I wanted to disappear into some kind of illness. Luckily, along the street there was a basement coffee shop, "The Artist." I took a seat there and ripped out one by one the pages of a poetry book that I had bought the day before. I grew frightened. A waitress filled my glass with water. I felt like plunging my nose into it and dying. It tasted salty. Is it sea water? Or have so many people already plunged their noses into it that it's full of snot? I grew frightened. Being alive seemed to be like repeating words someone had already spoken. I sighed and my breath emerged steaming white. Obviously someone inside me was chain-smoking.

One Day We Went to the Bank

One day we went to the bank.
Holding hands firmly, my sweetheart and I opened an account.
Behind our backs, the wings of the glass doors swung.
The bank is staying put, not flying away.
My sweetheart and I feel content.
Dreams have various shapes.
Giggling, we share cigarettes.
The bank's only etiquette is No Smoking.
Somehow it seems that our being in love
is a joke we're playing on the world. Murmuring,
Love, love, love, we leave the bank.
There are no feathers in the wings of the glass doors.
As we light up once we're outside the door,
my sweetheart is still giggling.
She says, Now we belong in the future,
We became adults in the future.
My sweetheart teaches me.
As I nod my head, my heart aches.
A moment before, a bankrupt bird went flying away.
Pitter-patter,
raindrops like feathers are falling.
One day, we'll have a lot of money.

Then, That Day, Walks

It was really bitter winter then.
We went for very many walks.
That day, heavy snow had fallen.
A lake bearing snowdrifts on just a thin layer of ice,
foot prints remembering dirty ground,
a small gray dot at the end of the road
was a big dog waiting for us.
In the park a famous singer was buried.
"A certain warmth will embrace the world."
His song brought him dazzling fame
but the grave was covered with an atrocity of dead flowers.
That day, the heavy snow stopped
and the piled-up snow gradually added to the ice's thickness.
The lake felt less concerned
about the next snowfall but
then our weak hearts
cracked as we kept thinking about the future.
Then ours was such a short-lived love.
We went for many walks.
That day, heavy snow fell then stopped.
That day, we came back home following the big dog.
It was our last walk.
We didn't know that then,

Inheritance

At our age we can strut along the street with cigarettes in our mouths. Avoiding the eyes of the elderly, carelessly tensing muscles to puff out the smoke, frequently flicking the ash off to show how bright we are .... But we have to be careful. Father's generation was a cigarette butt that had burned down too fast.

It was the year of the flood. Father's *World of Thinking* was fished out bloated and went moldy before it was dry. I remember the verse from Goethe I once found between the pages of an old book. "Over all hilltops is rest."

Life shakes dozens of times until it finds balance. Those who collapse in the process collapse completely. What might it take for them to stand up again? A revolution? Father, are you still lying there with an empty IV drip in your arm?

My legs are trapped in the pavement blocks. Someone is inhaling me so brutally, who is it? I stand there, musing. At our age, life goes on after suffering several total blackouts. A realization at last, fluttering like the curtain's fringe at the end of a act. Father, now I am grown up and strut along the street, I realize that I am one of the many rootlets of soliloquies you left behind!

Father, When I Recall Our Old Home

The ceiling of this room is low. How vulgar it is
if you can touch the ceiling without even jumping.
Cherishing the ceiling's allure through the window,
a cloud passes by.

When Father came home from work, he used to open his bag
and pour a bag-shaped mass of air onto the floor.
Wow, amazing! The children's unrestrained cries!
Sometimes, when I recall our old home,
bullets of memory and oblivion,
zoom, brushing past both cheeks, back and forth!

It seems as if there's a deep cliff hidden in our home's main bedroom.
At its foot lies ground that can be reached or can't be reached.
If I look back, my sister is way behind and yet farther behind is
    Mother,
and farther behind still is the far behind of the limitless
and farfarfarther behind is just the wall of the wardrobe.
Father died leaning against that wall,
midway between sitting and standing.
Father's left hand.
was grasping the satellite TV's remote control.

Father, who went fishing with boiled potatoes as bait,
who lay there with an empty IV drip,
who looked really handsome when very young,
Father, deceased posterity of the Cheongsong Shim clan.
While writing the ancestral tablet, I wept bitterly,
Father, why
are you doing art now you're dead?

Our old home's basement is my favorite place.
A place I can escape to, a place I have already returned to,
even if I intend not to return.
A place where peace is running well, like the Rinnai Boiler.

Alone beneath the low ceiling,
my back pressed hard against the back of the sofa,
I am peeping out at the swarming future low as it comes crawling
    low.

Somewhere in this house our whole family, even with no news,
must be doing well, I believe, no doubts.

Escape Route

As I leave the house, a kid is scribbling something on the wall. I decide to stand beside him and watch quietly. "Yeong-cheol says he loves Mi-yeong. Asshole. Mi-yeong's mine." The kid notices me, gets flustered, then runs away fast. He dashes straight ahead so fast that he seems to get smaller and smaller right in front of me.

Looking closely, there's a pile of broken bits of chalk at the foot of the wall. The kid had really been putting all his strength into writing. I bend over and smear my fingers with the powder. Asshole. Mi-yeong's mine. ... Such gentle hatred.

There's a loud rattling noise, as if there had been an empty lunch box in his bag. The kid has already disappeared around the corner but I can still hear the sound. Does shame go on rattling like that for a long time? As I move away, I suddenly notice how a great many rays of light, all fleeing in the same direction, are falling to the ground as black shadows.

Home Withdrawing

Not a running away from home, not a leaving home for good.
I was standing quite still before the door
when home simply slowly withdrew.
Therefore
my present state is a time of wandering,
wandering is my only circumstance.

Mother tells me to speak English now.
She says it was father's last testament.
'Honey, don't shed no tears,'
but the tears will not stop.
A weird dance and a wicked woman are stuck inside my body.
To extract that dance, that woman, I sang incessantly,
many twists and turns blossomed in my mind.

Not a running away from home, not a leaving home for good.
Home simply left me forever.
Therefore
I am standing on the site of home with only the garden left.
I am humming a ballad for the gardener.
On each petal, a precise beauty is gathered.
In my breast, a stubborn resolution has settled.

Above the far-away horizon,
flickering, minute as a bean,
shining like the evening star,
my old home.

Losing a Hometown

The day before Lunar New Year's Day, with mom and aunt, I am eating steamed monkfish in a shabby neighborhood restaurant. With no husband, no father, calling today a holiday feels wretched. When I call out 'Father' inside myself, sorrow bursts like a sea squirt, making a corner of my heart burn. Peeping into a small room to the back of the restaurant, I find it's a gambling den, of the kind I've only heard of, guys whose hometown has become their sworn enemy, a so-called roaring gambling den, a so-called land of taciturn ruination, their abject everyday seems to have absolutely nothing and everything to do with my mom and aunt's misfortune. Set between the two chattering women, sucking fish bones clean, I'm the odd man out. As I sip a cup of coffee from the vending machine, a kind of dessert, free because it's a holiday, I dimly glimpse through the crack of the door clenched hands with bulging muscles, playing cards being turned over, slapped down, sending covert glances like fish bones. Then, after finishing the meal, we drop in at Aunt's house, groping our way down the alleys of Hapjeong-dong with the help of dim memory, and this being the day before Lunar New Year's Day, there's a giving and taking of salted roes, dumplings, dried persimmons, one by one, one here, one there, I see mom and aunt spread an utterly delicious feast on the floor. On the way home after packing it all up, we hear words of wisdom on the traffic broadcast: There are no shortcuts on the journey back to your hometown; straight ahead, straight ahead is the only way." So mom and I head straight down the southern highway, turn off at Pangyo Interchange, head for Bundang. This is unmistakably the road to lost hometowns. No husband, no father, no grandfather, no grandmother. Toward the land of lost hometowns, mom and I, honk-honk, honk-honk, today and tomorrow go speeding on endlessly.

A Letter

Today as ever nothing changes here.
The sun rises and sets glowing red as shame.
I am living in a daze as usual.
Memories of a wasted youth
sometimes burst into tears inside my head
but I just smile,
since I was born destined to smile, I smile.
Once I smile,
the fierce past turns meek as a lamb.

Recently so many words have been coming to mind. Last night
I wrote in my diary:
A series of mistakes is
like dividing a deadly error several times.
After writing that,
I smiled.
Language is peaceful in form,
so that the most terrible confession makes a happy dream.

I cannot remember
what I dreamed last night
but I firmly believe it was a happy dream.

I feel so pathetic,
but now life's agony has become a genre,
its narrative development is very clear.
Since I only enjoy darkness,
I quietly urge the light my eyes dislike,
Would you mind growing dark?
then close my eyes, and so I spend my days.

At this moment outside the window
happiness is fluttering pettily
like an outdated advertisement.
On seeing how the roads beneath it have forgotten their essence
and become so crowded,
the pages of my mind crumple
and I groan

Probable, Very Probable

As if repeating an old habit, I gaze at the darkness outside the window. You ask, Why are you staring so long at the darkness? I answer, I didn't know it was darkness. Then you ask, Now you know it's darkness why are you still looking at it? I answer, Right now I am dreaming. Staring over my shoulder at the darkness, you say, Not at all, you are wide awake. It's just that too much solitude has carved a dreaming expression on your face.

Tonight, one in ten may leave for somewhere and one in ten may be very lonely. Then one in ten may sob. If I think of the probability that you and I may part tonight ($=0.1 \times 0.1 \times 0.1$), my face becomes pale like the surface of the moon stuck high up there like a white coin in the distant darkness. I just want to curl up in the euphemistic inside of time, whose beginning and end are vague, and fall asleep. Now I forget whether I am man or woman and am falling into anguish, mere anguish.

Like all sick dogs and all beginners, I am extremely awkward in front of destiny. I embraced you for a very long time but my heart refused rapture and only fiercely hammered in melancholy foreboding at the very center of my breast. Coincidence is like a moment when destiny hesitates for a second. At that very moment you and I met under a different destiny. But even if coincidence and destiny are entangled like a Mobius strip, what does it matter? Now we are being scattered in every direction like grains of sands before each other's eyes.

You give off a stench of night fog. Your gaze seems to visit inland wetlands in darkness over my shoulder before it reaches my eyes. You say, You are like a wretched book with the pages out of order from the very start. I close my eyes, sunk in shame. And I ask, Here are lies about everything and truths about things of no matter. Which of the two will be less sad? Which will be laid on immortality's bed in some distant future? The probability is half and half. Is not probability's dark algorithm composed of numbers that hide their tragic status?

I opened my eyes, Have you left? You left and are not here. As if repeating an old habit, I gaze at the darkness in front of my eyes that has been made much deeper by your absence. In the order of things, now is the time to sob and weep.

The Last Game of Tennis with Her

My imagination is not heartless; it hangs one or two strands of dream shadow on the bush where tails of sorrow are dimly seen. Not knowing on which they should concentrate between breathing in and breathing out, asthmatic days go flying between the narrow cracks of the universe like meteors. Irrespective of whether god is dead or not, only songs flowing from earphones send urgent messages to a world with no salvation. (No contents). I emerge after bowing before the Buddha, and the thousand-years-old pine tree standing on the hillside is as pathetic as a failed joke. A nun standing beside me says the crying sound is a crow's, but when I looked up, the age when they used to say it was the hermit with the finest voice had long gone by, so just consider it the boundless sky and go to sleep quickly. I am still secretly attached to sorrow, so words like magnolia, cat, glimmer block my way to self-conceit like an aged prostitute, Except for that, I walk along cheerfully in a dignified manner but I cannot help it, my tears keep flowing miraculously. I received my driver's license when I was well past thirty. Mother praises me, How well you drive, then weeps. Perhaps she's thinking of my deceased father. Sorrow is piling up in multiple layers between folder pages, but office workers merrily head for a karaoke room after working overtime. My sense of being grows infinitely dim when your favorite song is the same as mine, there is no hidden meaning in my resignation letter, I just hope you enjoy the soft fibers of sadness, brooding on that resolve. A few days before losing my job, on the way out after playing tennis with the woman I love I shout, Marry me. Sending a wonderful backhand volley, she jumps over the net, comes close, and whispers: Everything will soon be over. Don't you realize, it's match point.

Floating Words

Words are floating around. Among streets, among buildings, among bridges, in the floating words is news of my ex-wife or the unknown language of a flower. Outside the window, white ants are moving from landscape to landscape, nibbling at perspectives. For some time now, if I step into a painting, it tears. Where have all the landscapes gone that used to save me? Since the 1960's, God has been pretending to be dead. Since the 1960's, stress has been raised to the rank of those gods whose name ends in 's' such as Dionysus or Zeus. Now there's no prophecy that makes hearts flutter. Those already divorced still have a lot more divorces to come, every day seems to be another age, a picnic of innumerable changes. Intending to roll Gimbap, on account of rage the result is a rice ball. It's scary. The word 'objective' is every word's enemy. A few floating words joined together properly turn into the key to a different world. Still there's no salvation. I hear some god or other recently qualified as a chef. He spends all day making Dongpo pork and lives saying, 'It is finished, that looks very nice.' Words are floating around, among all the gaps and openings, as if sliding, swimming. Quibbling over the floating words, I often cry in front of people. At first, in front of one or two, but now I often cry in front of ten or twenty. My final goal is to cry in front of a record hundred people. A woman among them will hold me tight. I will love her, make love to her, marry her, and divorce her. If I shake a long-kept diary, countless, minute, trivial words fall out from between the pages and float in the air, lightly, buoyantly. Faced with beauty without salvation, again today I ache helplessly.

Treading on Footprints, I Head for the Future

They turn their backs first of all.
The dearest things
aimed their guns at memories.
Stay right where you are, guys.
If you want to live, die rather.
Disgusting. Sickening. Why
are things that are said to be eternal all like that?
I killed nine out of the ten longevity symbols,
I can't remember which one was left.
Is it a former sweetheart or an ex-wife,
or my footprints left beside them both?
They disappear first of all.
The things I loved most
turned memories inside out and all was just pitch black,

I become uglier day by day.
I smell bad.
Treading on footprints, I head for the future.
Let's live by the river, blistered feet!

About the Author

Shim Bo-Seon was born in Seoul in 1970, studied sociology at Seoul National University, and received his PhD from Columbia University, New York. He made his debut in the Chosun Ilbo Annual Spring Literary Contest in 1994 and published his first collection, *Seulpeumi opneun sip o cho* (Fifteen Seconds without Sorrow), in 2008. This collection was followed by *Nunape opneun saram* (Someone Not in Sight) in 2011 and Geueurin yesul (Smoked Art) in 2013. He is currently a professor of Culture and Art Management at Kyung-Hee Cyber University. He is a member of the Twenty-First Century Prospect Writer's Group.

Photograph of the author by Eun-You.
Used by permission.

About the Translators

Chung Eun-Gwi is Associate Professor of the Department of English Literature at Hankuk University of Foreign Studies, Seoul. She received her Ph.D in the Poetics Program, State University of New York at Buffalo, in 2005. Her publications include articles, translations, poems, and reviews in various journals, including *In/Outside: English Studies in Korea, Comparative Korean Studies, World Literature Today, Cordite*, and *Azalea*

Born in England in 1942, Brother Anthony of Taizé has lived in Korea since 1980. He is currently Emeritus Professor, English Department, Sogang University, and Chair-Professor, International Creative Writing Center, Dankook University. He has published more than thirty volumes of translated Korean poetry, as well as translations of several Korean novels, for which he has received a number of awards. He has published ten volumes of work by Ko Un, as well as recent volumes of work by Lee Si-Young and Kim Soo-bok. His Korean name is An Sonjae.

Free Verse Editions

Edited by Jon Thompson

13 ways of happily by Emily Carr
Between the Twilight and the Sky by Jennie Neighbors
Blood Orbits by Ger Killeen
The Bodies by Chris Sindt
The Book of Isaac by Aidan Semmens
Canticle of the Night Path by Jennifer Atkinson
Child in the Road by Cindy Savett
Condominium of the Flesh by Valerio Magrelli, trans. by Clarissa Botsford
Contrapuntal by Christopher Kondrich
Country Album by James Capozzi
The Curiosities by Brittany Perham
Current by Lisa Fishman
Dismantling the Angel by Eric Pankey
Divination Machine by F. Daniel Rzicznek
Erros by Morgan Lucas Schuldt
Fifteen Seconds without Sorrow by Shim Bo-Seon, translated by Chung Eun-Gwi
    and Brother Anthony of Taizé
The Forever Notes by Ethel Rackin
The Flying House by Dawn-Michelle Baude
Instances: Selected Poems by Jeongrye Choi, translated by Brenda Hillman, Wayne
    de Fremery, & Jeongrye Choi
The Magnetic Brackets by Jesús Losada, translated by Michael Smith & Luis
    Ingelmo
A Map of Faring by Peter Riley
No Shape Bends the River So Long by Monica Berlin & Beth Marzoni
Pilgrimly by Siobhán Scarry
Physis by Nicolas Pesque, translated by Cole Swensen
Poems from above the Hill & Selected Work by Ashur Etwebi, translated by Brenda
    Hillman & Diallah Haidar
The Prison Poems by Miguel Hernández, translated by Michael Smith
Puppet Wardrobe by Daniel Tiffany
Quarry by Carolyn Guinzio
remanence by Boyer Rickel
Signs Following by Ger Killeen
Split the Crow by Sarah Sousa
Spine by Carolyn Guinzio
Spool by Matthew Cooperman

www.ingramcontent.com/pod-product-compliance
Lightning Source LLC
Chambersburg PA
CBHW022038090426
42741CB00007B/1119